Perry's Simplified Rules of Order

Darryl W. Perry
F. Mac Perry

FREE PRESS PUBLICATIONS

ISBN: 978-1-938357-38-1
Open Library: OL51715368M
LCCN: 2024911289

First edition: July 2024

Published by Free Press Publications
FPP.cc

FPP.cc
FREE PRESS PUBLICATIONS

Table of Contents

Introduction

Rules of Order are intended to help a group have orderly meetings while also allowing members to participate in discussion and decision making. Rules of Order are not meant to be used as a weapon by a learned class against the layperson.

Perry's Simplified Rules of Order (**PRO**) is designed to be easy to understand and use, while eliminating the ability to use the rules to obstruct a meeting.

As with all rules of order, PRO should be used where a body's By-laws or Constitution are silent. Additionally, organizations are urged to make their bylaws comprehensive and easy to understand.

As a work licensed under Creative Commons BY-SA 4.0, you are allowed to copy, redistribute, remix, transform, and build upon the material in any medium or format for any purpose, even commercially with the requirements that any work should:

- include the statements:
  - "This work is based upon *Perry's Simplified Rules of Order* (**PRO**) by Darryl W. Perry & F. Mac Perry."
  - "Neither this work nor the author(s) is endorsed by Darryl W. Perry or F. Mac Perry.";
- not remove any of the rules in PRO;
- retain the name *Perry's Simplified Rules of Order* (**PRO**) and the title shall be appended with the name of the person or entity, and may be abbreviated **PRO-[initials]**.

0. Vocabulary

0.1. Whenever a member makes a motion, call, challenge, or point of order the Chair shall not deem it to be out of order simply because the member used the wrong term.

0.2. For example:

0.2.1. "division" or "motion for division" shall be understood to be a request to divide;

0.2.2. "point of information" or "point of inquiry" shall be understood to be a request for information; and

0.2.3. "motion to suspend the rule to/and [fill in the blank]" shall be understood to mean a motion to suspend the rules to consider the item.

0.3. If the Chair is unsure what motion the member is trying to make, the Chair shall ask for clarification so that the member is able to fully participate in the meeting.

1. Authority

1.1. When adopted as a parliamentary authority, PRO does not supersede any rules adopted in an organization's bylaws, constitution, standing rules, or other governing document.

1.2. An organization adopting PRO is encouraged to use the following language:

1.2.1. Perry's Simplified Rules of Order (PRO) shall be the parliamentary authority for all matters of procedure not specifically covered by our [insert here all governing documents]. The rules of order may be suspended for a specific purpose, if approved by two thirds (2/3) of those present provided a quorum is present.

2. Call to order

2.1. The Chair, or their designee, is responsible for calling a meeting to order. A meeting should only be called to order once the Chair determines a quorum is present and at/after the scheduled start time.

2.2. A meeting shall never be called to order absent a quorum or before the scheduled start time.

3. Agenda

3.1. Adopting an agenda

3.1.1. A proposed meeting agenda shall always be provided before the start of the meeting.

3.1.2. Proposed agendas must be adopted by majority vote.

3.2. Amending an agenda

3.2.1. A motion to amend the proposed agenda does not require a second, and requires a 2/3 vote in favor or may be adopted with unanimous consent.

3.2.2. Amendments to an adopted agenda do require a second, and requires a 2/3 vote in favor or may be adopted with unanimous consent.

4. Motions

4.1. Main motions

4.1.1. Any agenda item shall be a main motion and will not require a second to be considered by the body. Agenda items originating from a committee may have a recommendation of ought to pass or inexpedient to pass. All main motions brought by a member of the body will require a second to be considered.

4.2. Amendments

4.2.1. Any main motion may be amended by a 2/3 vote. Motions to amend require a second and should be germane to, and not negate, the main motion.

4.2.2. If a main motion is a modification of an existing document (eg bylaws, constitution, standing rules, or platform), any motion to amend should only relate to the proposed change (i.e. if a motion proposes to rewrite the first sentence of a paragraph, an amendment should only relate to that sentence).

4.2.3. Any member may request a ruling from the Chair on whether the amendment is in order.

4.3. Secondary amendment

4.3.1. A motion to amend may be amended according to the same rules as amending a main motion; and shall be called the secondary amendment.

4.4. Tertiary amendment

4.4.1. An amendment to a secondary amendment is never in order.

4.4.2. The secondary amendment shall be voted on before consideration of additional amendments.

4.5. Substitute motion

4.5.1. A substitute motion shall be considered a secondary amendment; and shall not be amended.

4.5.2. A substitute motion shall be voted on before consideration of additional amendments, substitute motions are subject to the same rules as motions to amend.

4.6. Division

4.6.1. Any motion that has multiple parts shall be divided upon request. No second is needed for a request to divide; and does not require approval from the body.

4.6.2. An objection to such a request shall require a 2/3 vote to prevent the request to divide.

4.7. Table or postpone

4.7.1. A motion may be postponed or placed on the table. Any motion to postpone should include the time at which it will be considered (eg "motion to postpone until after agenda item 5", or "motion to postpone until the next meeting"). Such motion requires a second; and is debatable. If a motion to table or postpone fails by majority vote, then the previous motion will be taken up.

4.7.2. Any item placed on the table may be removed with a majority vote. If the body dissolves upon adjourning, items may not be postponed to a future meeting or later removed from the table.

4.8. Reconsideration

4.8.1. Any member who voted on the prevailing side of a main motion, motion to postpone, or an amendment to a motion that has not already been subject to a vote of reconsideration may make a motion to reconsider.

4.8.2. A motion to reconsider requires 2/3 vote to be reconsidered.

4.8.3. If the motion to reconsider passes, the item becomes a main motion.

4.9. Suspending the rules

4.9.1. A member may move to suspend the rules for the purpose of bringing up an item of business out of order i.e. at a time other than the allotted time in the agenda or an item not on the agenda, or to amend the process by which specific business is conducted.

4.9.1.1. An organization’s bylaws or constitution may not be suspended.

4.9.2. A motion to suspend the rules requires a second, is always debatable, and requires a 2/3 vote.

4.9.3. If a motion to suspend the rules passes, then the item of business shall be considered by the body.

4.10. Withdrawing a motion

4.10.1. A member who made a motion may withdraw the motion prior to the vote.

5. Calling a vote

5.1. Any member may call a vote (call the question). If the Chair determines further debate is prudent, then such a call shall be voted upon by the body; and shall require 2/3 vote or may be adopted with unanimous consent.

5.1.1. A call of the question does not require a second.

5.2. The Chair should only call a vote after determining there is no need for more discussion.

6. Debate

6.1. Discussion of motions should be related to the motion on the floor, and all members should be able to speak within reason.

6.2. The Chair should, to the best of their ability, alternate speakers in favor and those opposed.

6.3. Filibustering is not allowed, and the Chair shall restore order if a member is filibustering or acting in a dilatory manner.

6.4. Debate should be civil, and members shall refrain from personal attacks.

7. Votes

7.1. Each member is entitled to one vote.

7.2. A body may adopt a rule requiring all members present to vote.

7.3. Except for votes for elections, votes may be taken by asking for unanimous consent (i.e. without objection), via voice vote, or by show of hands or rising vote.

7.4. Upon request and a second by at least 5% of attending members, a vote shall be conducted by secret ballot. Secret ballots should be used for elections of candidates.

7.5. Any voting that uses electronic ballots should include a method of human verification and tabulation of votes.

8. Points of order & rulings of the Chair

8.1. Point of order

8.1.1. A point of order may be raised to request a ruling from the Chair if a member thinks an action violates the rules or otherwise disturbs the order of the meeting.

8.1.1.1. A point of order may be raised prior to formal recognition by the Chair; however, the Chair shall immediately recognize the member raising the point of order.

8.1.1.2. After a point of order has been raised, the Chair shall either affirm the point of order or give a reason for denying the point of order.

8.1.2. Points of order take precedence over all other motions, except challenges to the ruling of the Chair.

8.2. Challenge to a ruling of the Chair

8.2.1. Any ruling of the Chair may be challenged by any member and does not require a second. The member making the challenge (challenger) shall briefly state the nature of the challenge (i.e. cite the rule or bylaw that supports their challenge).

8.2.2. The Chair shall be allowed to speak in support of their ruling immediately after the ruling has been challenged and immediately before the vote.

8.2.3. The challenger shall be allowed to speak further to their challenge after the Chair's initial remarks.

8.2.4. Not more than two additional members shall be allowed to speak in favor of the ruling or the challenge.

8.2.5. Discussion on a challenge to the ruling of the Chair shall be relevant only to the ruling or the challenge. During debate on a challenge, the Chair shall not preside, and the Acting Chair shall prevent filibuster and dilatory speech.

8.2.6. After the Chair's closing remarks the Acting Chair shall call the vote by stating "If you support the ruling of the Chair vote 'Yes.' If you support the challenge to the ruling vote 'No'. All in favor of the ruling, say 'Yes.'"
"All in favor of the challenge, say 'No.'"

8.2.7. A majority vote is required to sustain the ruling of the Chair.

8.2.8. After the Acting Chair gives the results of the vote, the Chair shall resume presiding over the meeting.

8.2.9. A challenge to the ruling of the Chair must be dispensed with before any other business may resume.

8.3. Orders of the day

8.3.1. Orders of the day is a special point of order that requires no recognition or subsequent ruling of the Chair.

8.3.2. When a member calls orders of the day, the body shall immediately proceed to a vote on all pending motions; and move to the scheduled agenda item.

8.3.3. Orders of the day can only be called when the body is behind schedule, otherwise the Chair shall state that the call for orders of the day is out of order.

8.4. Request for information

8.4.1. Whenever a motion is up for a vote, a member may request information from the Chair. The question should only be seeking clarification of the motion. Any debate disguised as a request for information should not be allowed.

9. Disruptions

9.1. If a member is filibustering or acting in a dilatory manner, fails to comply with a ruling of the Chair, or is disrupting business; the body may, by a majority, vote to remove the member from the meeting.

10. Quorum

10.1. A quorum is required for a body to conduct business, and a should be at least a majority of the body.

10.2. If a member is filling more than one seat on the body, each seat will count towards quorum; however, the member will only be allowed to fill a single seat for purposes of voting and should declare that seat at the beginning of the meeting.

10.3. If quorum is lost during a meeting, the meeting must immediately adjourn, without voting on any pending motions.

11. Types of Meetings

11.1. Regular Meetings

11.1.1. A regular meeting is typically held at a regular interval for the purpose of discussing day-to-day business.

11.2. Annual Meetings and Conventions

11.2.1. An annual meeting or convention is a meeting in which members, shareholders, or delegates of an organization meet to conduct certain business that is outside the scope of a regular meeting.

11.2.2. During an annual meeting or convention, the meeting belongs to the body and the body is able to conduct all business that is not prohibited by the organization's governing documents.

11.2.3. The body typically dissolves upon adjourning a convention.

11.3. Electronic meetings

11.3.1. A body may choose to meet in person or virtually using electronic means of communication. Electronic meetings are subject to the same rules as in-person meetings.

12. Adjourn

12.1. Meetings may be adjourned to a time certain or adjourned *sine die* (with no appointed date for resumption).

12.2. If the agenda specifies a time for adjournment, the Chair shall move to a vote on all pending motions at the appointed time and the meeting shall adjourn.

12.3. A motion to extend time shall be considered a motion to amend the agenda; and shall not be debatable.

12.4. If the agenda does not specify a time for adjournment, and all business from the agenda has been considered, the Chair may ask for unanimous consent to adjourn.

12.5. Any member may make a motion to adjourn, and such motion shall require 2/3 vote or may be adopted with unanimous consent.

12.6. A motion to adjourn to a time certain is only debatable with regards to the time of resumption.

12.7. A member must be recognized to make a motion to adjourn, and the motion to adjourn does not take precedence over points of order.

Example of a Meeting under PRO

The following is a fictional scenario showing how to use PRO.

C: Chair **VC:** Vice Chair

M: Member **S:** Secretary

C: The time is now 9am, and it appears we have a quorum. I call this meeting to order.

C: Is there a motion to approve the agenda?

M1: Motion to amend the agenda to have the Treasurer's report before the Secretary's report.

C: The motion to amend the proposed agenda does not require a second. Is there any need for debate or an objection to this amendment?

C: Hearing none, the amendment is adopted. Is there a motion to approve the agenda?

M1: Motion to approve the agenda as amended.

C: The agenda needs a majority vote to be adopted, all in favor say "Yes"; those opposed say "No."

C: The agenda is adopted.

C: The first agenda item is approval of the Minutes from the last meeting. This item does not require a second. Is there objection to approving the Minutes from the last meeting?

M2: Objection

C: There is objection. Is there any debate?

M2: My name is misspelled on page 2 of the Minutes. I move to correct this error.

C: Names will be corrected in the Minutes without objection.

[pause to give members a chance to object]

C: Is there any further debate?

[wait for people to respond]

C: Hearing none, the Minutes are adopted.

C: The first item on the agenda is adopting a resolution to recognize the contributions of John Smith to our organization.

M1: I'd like to make a motion to amend this resolution to also recognize the Bill Johnson

M2: Second

C: The motion to amend has been seconded. Is there debate on this motion? Hearing none, is there objection to the amendment?

C: Hearing none, the amendment is adopted and is now the main motion. Is there any further debate?

M3: I request a rising vote.

C: The member has requested a rising vote, is there objection?

M4: Objection. I have a petition signed by the requisite number of members to have a secret ballot on all main motions.

C: Has the petition been given to the Secretary?

S: Yes, I have received the petition.

C: This will be a secret ballot. Will the Vice Chair and Secretary be willing to tally the votes?

VC: Yes

S: I'm willing as long as no business is conducted during the tabulation, since I need to keep Minutes.

C: The body will be at ease during the tabulation.

C: Is there any further discussion on the motion? <pause> Hearing none, please use Ballot #1 in your packet to vote on the resolution to recognize the contributions of John Smith and Bill Johnson to our organization. A "Yes" vote is in support of the resolution, and a "No" vote is in opposition to the resolution.

M1: Mr. Chair, request for information.

C: What is your request?

M1: To pass, does the resolution require a majority of members present or a majority of the vote?

C: We have not adopted a rule requiring members present to vote, so the resolution only requires a majority of the vote.

M1: I motion to amend the standing rules to require members present to vote.

C: We're in the middle of another motion, that motion as stated is out of order unless you move to suspend the rules to take up the motion.

M1: I would like to do that.

C: There is a motion to suspend the rules for the purpose of consideration of a motion to amend the standing rules to require members present to vote. Is there a second?

C: The motion dies for lack of a second.

C: We are using Ballot #1 to vote on the resolution to recognize the contributions of John Smith and Bill Johnson to our organization. A "Yes" vote is in support of the resolution, and a "No" vote is in opposition to the resolution. Please hold your ballot up for the Tellers to see that you have finished completing your ballot.

C: The body will be at ease until ballots are counted.

[ballots are tabulated]

C: The ballots have been tabulated, does the Secretary have the results?

S: Yes, the results are 37 "Yes" votes, and 2 "No" votes.

C: Thank you, the motion passes.

C: The next item on the agenda is the Treasurer's report, followed by the Secretary's report.

[Treasurer and Secretary give reports]

M2: Orders of the Day!

C: Orders of the Day have been called, and we are 15 minutes behind schedule. We will now recess for lunch and return at 12:45.

[Recess for lunch]

C: The body will come to order. The time is 12:45, the meeting will now resume with the next item on the agenda.

M3: Point of Order!

C: What's the Point of Order?

M3: The meeting went into recess without hearing the Vice Chair's report, and the first item of business after lunch is officer elections.

C: I believe you've made a Request for Information regarding the next item on the agenda, is that correct?

M3: Yes.

C: Before lunch, Orders of the Day were called. In accordance with PRO, we will now proceed to election of officers.

M3: When will we hear the Vice Chair's report?

C: There is not currently a time set for Vice Chair's report.

M3: Is there a way to hear that report before voting on officers?

C: That would require a motion to amend the agenda. Since the agenda has already been approved, a motion to amend the agenda would need a 2/3 vote.

M3: Can I make that motion?

C: You may.

M3: Motion to amend the agenda to hear the Vice Chair's report before officer elections.

C: Is there a second?

M1: SECOND!

C: The motion has been moved and seconded. Is there any need for debate or an objection to this motion?

M4: Request for Information.

C: Is your request related to the pending motion?

M4: Yes. Is this motion considered a main motion or an amendment?

C: Since the agenda has already been approved, this is a main motion.

M4: Thank you, and I'd like to remind the Chair that a petition was submitted this morning to have a secret ballot on all main motions.

C: Thank you for the reminder. Is there any more debate on the motion to amend the agenda to hear the Vice Chair's report before officer elections?

C: Hearing none, please take ballot #2 from your packet. A "Yes" vote will amend the agenda to hear the Vice Chair's report before officer elections, and a "No" vote will have us move immediately to officer elections. Please hold your ballot up for the Tellers to see that you have finished completing your ballot.

C: The body will be at ease until ballots are counted.

[ballots are tabulated]

C: The ballots have been tabulated, does the Secretary have the results?

S: Yes, the results are 12 "Yes" votes, and 22 "No" votes.

C: Thank you, the motion fails, and we will now proceed to election of officers. The officers up for election this year are Secretary, Treasurer and Vice Chair. Nominations are now open.

[proceeds to nominations]

M2: Request for Information.

C: We're in the middle of nominating candidates, is your request related to the nomination or election?

M2: Yes. Do we require officers to be elected by majority or plurality?

C: Our rules require a majority to be elected.

M2: Motion to suspend the rules to elect the person who gets the most votes.

C: There is a motion to suspend the rules. Is there a second?

M3: Second.

C: The motion has been seconded. Is there any debate or objection to suspending the rules to hear a motion to elect the person who gets the most votes?

M4: Objection, there's a petition to have a secret ballot on all main motions.

C: Are you objecting to the suspension of the rules?

M4: No. I'm stating that we need to have a secret ballot on this motion.

C: A suspension of the rules is not a main motion. The main motion will only be debated and voted on if this body votes to suspend the rules. Is there any debate or objection to suspending the rules to hear a motion to elect the person who gets the most votes?

C: Hearing none, the rules have been suspended to hear the motion to elect the person who gets the most votes. Is there any debate?

M2: May I speak to my motion?

C: You may.

M2: We are already behind schedule and with the number of candidates, it's likely we would need multiple rounds to elect officers with a majority of the vote. This motion will save time.

C: Is there any additional debate?

M5: I'd like to make a substitute motion. Is that in order?

C: A substitute motion would be in order.

M5: Motion to use approval voting while retaining the requirement for a majority to be elected.

C: Not everyone is familiar with approval voting. Can you briefly explain it?

M5: Yes, everyone is able to vote for as many candidates as they like. For instance, instead of only voting for Candidate A or Candidate C, you can vote for Candidates A & C or A & B, or A, B & C.

C: Thank you for the explanation. Is there a second?

M1: Second.

C: We have a motion and a substitute motion, both have been seconded. Is there any debate?

C: Hearing none, we will now vote on the substitute motion. If the substitute motion passes, it will become the main motion. Is there objection to adopting the substitute motion to use approval voting?

M3: Objection.

C: There is objection. To become the main motion, a substitute motion requires 2/3 vote. All in favor of adopting the substitute motion to use Bucklin voting for the officer election, say "Yes." [wait for people to respond] Those opposed say "No." [wait for people to respond]

C: The substitute motion was adopted and is now the main motion. Please use Ballot #3 in your packet to vote. A "Yes" vote is in support of the motion to use approval voting for election of officers, and a "No" vote will use the standard majority vote rules. Please hold your ballot up for the Tellers to see that you have finished completing your ballot.

C: The body will be at ease until ballots are counted.

[ballots are tabulated]

M4: Request for information.

C: Is the request related to this vote?

M4: Yes. Does this motion require a simple majority or 2/3 vote?

C: A main motion requires a simple majority.

M4: This motion was a suspension of the rules.

C: That's incorrect. The suspension of the rules was to hear the motion. The motion only needs a majority to pass.

M4: I challenge the ruling of the Chair.

C: What is the nature of your challenge?

M4: You stated that this motion was not a suspension of the rules and only requires a majority to pass. M2 stated "Motion to suspend the rules to elect the person who gets the most votes." That requires a 2/3 vote.

C: Our rules are clear that a suspension of the rules requires 2/3 vote in order to hear a motion. The motion then only requires a majority to pass. See 0.2.3 and 3.9 of PRO. The Vice Chair will now take the gavel.

M4: A motion to suspend the rules to do a thing requires 2/3 vote and is different than a motion to suspend the rules to hear a motion.

VC: Would anyone else like to speak to the ruling or to the challenge?

M1: The Chair made the correct ruling. Our rules are simple and easy to understand. M4 is being dilatory and disruptive.

VC: M1, comments should only be related only to the ruling or the challenge. Remarks directed at another member are out of order. Would anyone else like to speak to the ruling or to the challenge?

VC: The Chair may make their final remarks.

C: M4 is confusing our parliamentary rules with something more rigid. We adopted rules that allow for member participation without needing to remember rules from a book with several hundred pages.

VC: A majority vote is required to sustain the ruling of the Chair. If you support the Ruling of the Chair vote 'Yes.' If you support the challenge to the ruling vote No'. All in favor of the ruling, say 'Yes.' [wait for people to respond]

VC: All in favor of the challenge, say 'No.'

[wait for people to respond]

VC: The ruling of the Chair is sustained. They will now retake the gavel.

C: Thank you. Have the ballots been tabulated?

S: Yes, the ballots have been tabulated.

M2: Point of Order.

C: What's the Point of Order?

M2: My ballot wasn't collected by a teller before the challenge to your ruling.

C: Please bring your ballot to the Secretary. If anyone else's ballot wasn't collected before the challenge to the ruling of the Chair, please raise your hand. [wait for people to raise hands]

Could the tellers please collect the other ballots?

C: We will stand at ease until these additional ballots are counted.

[ballots are tabulated]

S: Chair, the additional ballots have been tabulated.

C: Thank you, what are the results?

S: There were 23 "Yes" votes and 16 "No" votes.

C: Thank you, the motion passes. We will use approval voting for officer elections. Are there any further nominations? [wait for people to speak]

C: Seeing no additional nominations, nominations are now closed. Please use ballot #4 to vote for vote for Secretary, ballot #5 for Treasurer and ballot #6 for Vice Chair. Please place a 1 next to your top choice candidate, a 2 for second choice, 3 for third, etc. Please raise your ballots for collection by the tellers. The body will be at ease while ballots are collected and tallied.

[ballots are collected and tabulated]

M4: Request for Information

C: What's your request?

M4: Can we hear the Vice Chair's report during voting?

C: That would require an amendment to the agenda, and that motion will not be entertained while ballots are still being collected. Additionally, this body has already voted down amending the agenda to hear that report before voting. The Chair requests that M4 refrain from further dilatory behavior. The body will remain at ease during voting.

M5: Can I make a motion to amend the agenda to hear Sally's presentation while ballots are counted instead of having her present after officer elections?

C: M5, that would require a suspension of the rules to be considered. However, because of the petition submitted this morning for secret ballots on all main motions, we would need the tellers to collect and tabulate votes on your motion while they're in the middle of counting ballots for the officer election.

M5: I was one of the signers of that petition and would like to remove my name from the petition.

C: Please stand at ease for a moment while I confer with the Secretary.

C: We have 43 members present, and the petition was submitted by 3 people which is over 5%. If you remove your name from the petition, then it drops below the 5% threshold meaning the vote can be a voice vote.

M5: Thank you, I'd like to make that motion.

C: The body will come to order. There is a motion to suspend the rules to consider amending the agenda to hear Sally's presentation during vote tabulation instead of after officer elections. Is there a second?

M1: Second.

C: Is there objection to suspending the rules to consider the motion? [wait for people to respond]

C: Hearing none, the motion on the floor is to amend the agenda to hear Sally's presentation while votes are being counted. The petition for secret ballot has fallen below the 5% threshold, and we will not be using a secret ballot. Is there any objection to amending the agenda to hear Sally's presentation while votes are being counted?

[wait for people to respond]

C: The motion passes without objection.

[Sally's presentation]

C: Have the votes been tabulated?

S: Yes, they have.

C: I will now read the results of the elections.

[Chair gives results of elections]

C: The next item on the agenda is scheduled to start in 15 minutes. The Chair will entertain a motion to either recess for 15 minutes or to move to the next agenda item.

M1: Motion to move the next agenda item.

M3: Second.

C: There is a motion and a second to move to the next agenda item, Membership recruitment. Is there any objection?

[wait for people to respond]

C: Hearing none, we will move to the next agenda item.

[Membership recruitment presentation]

C: We have reached the end of the agenda. Is there objection to adjourning?

[wait for people to respond]

C: The meeting is adjourned.

FAQ

1. How is PRO (*Perry's Simplified Rules of Order*) different from RONR (*Robert's Rules of Order Newly Revised*)?

PRO is tailored to simplify and clarify procedures for running a meeting. PRO focuses on flexibility and ease of use, accommodating modern meeting practices, including electronic meetings. While RONR is a comprehensive and widely used set of parliamentary procedures, it is rigid in nature and people who are more knowledgeable with the rules can manipulate a meeting.

2. Why create new rules of order?

New rules of order can simplify procedures, clarify ambiguities, and ensure the rules are easy to understand and use.

3. What is the purpose of using PRO?

The purpose of using PRO is to ensure meetings are conducted efficiently, fairly, and transparently. PRO aims to facilitate active participation, clear decision-making, and effective management of business during meetings.

4. How does the Chair handle incorrect terminology used by members?

If a member uses incorrect terminology, the Chair shall not deem the motion out of order simply for that reason. The Chair will interpret the member's intent and ask for clarification to ensure proper understanding of the motion and participation of the member.

5. What happens if the Chair is unsure about a motion being made?

If the Chair is unsure about a motion, they will ask the member for clarification. This ensures that the member's intent is understood and that they can fully participate in the meeting.

6. What constitutes a quorum, and why is it important?
A quorum is the minimum number of members required to be present for the body to conduct official business. It is typically a majority of the body. A quorum ensures that decisions are made with sufficient representation and legitimacy.

7. How should an agenda be adopted and amended?
A proposed meeting agenda should be provided before the meeting and must be adopted by a majority vote. A motion to amend the proposed agenda does not require a second while a motion to amend an approved agenda does require a second. Amendments to an agenda require a 2/3 vote or unanimous consent.

8. What are the rules for making and amending motions?
Main motions require a second to be considered unless they originate from the agenda. Amendments to motions require a second and a 2/3 vote to pass. Amendments must be germane to the main motion and can not negate the intent of the main motion. A secondary amendment may not be amended.

9. What are the rules for substitute motions?
A substitute motion is treated as a secondary amendment and cannot be further amended. It must be voted on before additional amendments or substitute motions may be brought. If a substitute motion is approved, it becomes the main motion.

10. What is the process for reconsidering a motion?
A motion to reconsider can be made by a member who voted on the prevailing side of the original motion, and requires a 2/3 vote to pass. If the motion to reconsider is approved, the item becomes a main motion.

11. How can the rules be suspended during a meeting?

A member may move to suspend the rules to bring up an item out of order, or to amend the process by which specific business is conducted. This motion requires a second, is debatable, and needs a 2/3 vote to pass. Debate on a motion to suspend the rules should only relate to suspension of the rules. If approved, the item will be considered by the body and subject to the rules of a main motion.

12. What is the protocol for calling a vote?

Any member may call a vote, or "Call the Question." If the Chair deems further debate necessary, the call to vote will itself be voted upon, requiring a 2/3 vote or unanimous consent. The Chair typically calls a vote when there is no need for more discussion.

13. How should debate be conducted to ensure fairness and civility?

Debate should be relevant to the motion on the floor. The Chair should alternate between speakers for and against the motion, prevent filibustering, and ensuring that all members can speak within reason. Personal attacks are not allowed.

14. What are the different methods of voting allowed?

Votes can be taken by unanimous consent (i.e. without objection), voice vote, show of hands, or rising vote. Secret ballots must be used upon request by at least 5% of attending members or for elections of candidates. Electronic ballots should include a method of human verification.

15. How are points of order and challenges to the Chair's rulings handled?

A point of order can be raised to address violations of rules or order disruptions. The Chair must immediately address it. Any ruling by the Chair can be challenged by any member without a second. The challenge is debated and voted upon, requiring a majority to sustain the Chair's ruling.

16. What actions can be taken if a member is disruptive during the meeting?

If a member is disruptive, filibustering, or not complying with the Chair's rulings, the body may vote by majority to remove the member from the meeting to restore order.

17. How are electronic meetings managed under these rules?

Electronic meetings are subject to the same rules as in-person meetings. The platform used should facilitate participation, voting, and debate according to the established rules.

18. What are the guidelines for adjourning a meeting?

Meetings may be adjourned to a specific time or *sine die* (without a set resumption date). The agenda may specify an adjournment time, and a motion to extend time can amend the agenda but is not debatable. A motion to adjourn to a time certain is only debatable with regards to the time of resumption.

Any member who is recognized to speak can make a motion to adjourn, requiring a 2/3 vote or unanimous consent.

19. How are motions to table or postpone handled?

A motion to table or postpone should include a time for reconsideration. It requires a second, is debatable, and requires a majority vote. If it fails, the original motion is taken up. Items on the table can be removed by a majority vote, but cannot be postponed to a future meeting if the body dissolves upon adjournment.

20. What does it mean to divide a motion, and how is it done?

Any motion with multiple parts may be divided into distinct parts for individual consideration. A request to divide does not need a second or approval from the body, though an objection to dividing requires a 2/3 vote to prevent it.

21. How does the Chair ensure that debate is balanced and orderly?

The Chair should alternate between speakers for and against the motion, prevent filibustering and dilatory actions, and maintain civility by ensuring debate stays relevant to the motion and free from personal attacks.

22. What are the consequences of losing quorum during a meeting?

If quorum is lost, the meeting must immediately adjourn without voting on any pending motions. Quorum is essential for the validity of any decisions made during the meeting.

23. Can a motion be withdrawn after it has been made?

Yes, the member who made the motion can withdraw it before it is voted on. This allows for flexibility and reconsideration if the motion is no longer deemed necessary.

24. What is the process for handling a request for information during a meeting?

A member may request information from the Chair regarding clarification of a motion. This should not be used to debate the motion and is intended purely for informational purposes.

25. How are votes by secret ballot conducted and verified?

Secret ballots are conducted upon request by at least 5% of attending members or for elections. Electronic ballots should include a method of human verification to ensure accuracy and transparency.

Summary of Perry's Simplified Rules of Order (PRO)

Designed for Simplicity

- **Concise Format**: The rules are only 17 pages long, ensuring they can be easily understood and applied.
- **Easy to Understand and Use**: PRO aims to simplify parliamentary procedure, making it accessible for all members, regardless of their familiarity with traditional rules.

Inclusivity and Participation

- **Less Formal:** Members can participate even if they use incorrect terminology, ensuring inclusivity and active participation from all members (Rule 0.1).
- **No Advantage for Rule Experts**: The rules are designed so that those more familiar with them do not have an advantage over newcomers (Rule 0.3).
- **Division of Complex Motions**: Any motion with multiple parts can be divided upon request without needing a second, simplifying the decision-making process (Rule 4.6.1).

Emphasis on Civility and Order

- **Civility in Debate**: The rules emphasize civility and limit filibustering to maintain orderly and respectful discussions (Rule 6.4).
- **Managing Disruptions**: Members who are disruptive may be removed by the body, ensuring that meetings can proceed smoothly and efficiently (Rule 9.1).

Consensus and Unanimous Consent

- **Consensus Building**: The rules emphasize reaching consensus and encourage unanimous consent where possible, promoting collective agreement and cooperation (Rule 7.3).

Governance and Adoption

- **Simplified Adoption**: PRO is simplified for adoption as the parliamentary authority, making it easy for organizations to integrate (Rule 1.2).
- **Respect for Existing Rules**: The rules emphasize not superseding bylaws or standing rules, respecting the organization's established governance structures (Rule 1.1).

Modern and Flexible

- **Electronic Meetings**: PRO explicitly states that electronic meetings are subject to the same rules as in-person meetings, providing flexibility for modern meeting formats (Rule 11.3).

Comparison with RONR

PRO	*RONR*
Designed to be easy to understand and use, aiming to simplify parliamentary procedure.	More comprehensive and detailed, covering a wide range of situations and procedures.
Only 13 pages of rules that can easily be understood.	Nearly 700 pages of rules that are complicated and can be hard to understand.
Those more familiar with the rules do not have an advantage over those who are not.	Those more familiar with the rules are able to manipulate a meeting.
Less formal, allowing members to participate even if they use incorrect terminology.	More formal, with specific language and procedures that must be followed strictly.
Simplifies the process by emphasizing civility and limiting filibustering.	Has detailed rules for debate, including specific time limits and decorum.
Any motion with multiple parts can be divided upon request without a second.	Requires a second and sometimes debate and a vote to divide a motion.
Explicitly states that electronic meetings are subject to the same rules as in-person meetings.	Provides guidelines for electronic meetings but generally assumes in-person meetings unless otherwise specified.

PRO	*RONR*
Emphasizes reaching consensus and encourages unanimous consent where possible.	Focuses more on majority rule and has detailed procedures for handling dissent and debate.
Simplified for adoption as the parliamentary authority and emphasizes not superseding bylaws or standing rules.	More detailed and extensive process for adopting rules and integrating them with existing governing documents.

Perry's Simplified Rules of Order Cheat Sheet
Motions

Action	Second needed?	Debatable	Amendable	Without Objection?	Majority
Approve Agenda	N	Y	Y	N	Y
Amendment to Proposed Agenda	N	Y	Y	Y	2/3
Amendment to Approved Agenda	Y	Y[1]	Y	Y	2/3
Main Motion from Agenda	N	Y	Y	Y	Y
Main Motion from Floor	Y	Y	Y	Y	Y
Amendment to Main Motion[2]	Y	Y	Y	Y	2/3
Amendment to Amendment	Y	Y	N	Y	2/3

[1] A motion to extend time is an amendment to an approved agenda and is not debatable.
[2] Amendments should be germane to the main motion.

Motions

Action	Second needed?	Debatable	Amendable	Without Objection?	Majority
Substitute Motion	Y	Y	N	Y	2/3
Table	Y	Y	N	Y	Y
Remove from Table	Y	Y	N	Y	Y
Postpone	Y	Y	N	Y	Y
Reconsider[3]	Y	Y	N	Y	2/3
Suspend the Rules	Y	Y	N	Y	2/3
Adjourn to time certain	N	Y[4]	Y	Y	2/3
Adjourn sine die	N	N	N	Y	2/3
Divide the question	N	Does not require approval from the body. Requires 2/3 votes to prevent the motion to divide.			
Secret Ballot	5% of body	Secret ballots should be used for elections of candidates. Any voting that uses electronic ballots should include a method of human verification and tabulation of votes.			

[3] Motion to Reconsider can only be brought by a member voting on the prevailing side.
[4] A motion to adjourn to a time certain is only debatable with regards to the time of resumption.

Perry's Simplified Rules of Order Cheat Sheet

Types of Points of Order

	Interrupting?	Purpose	Action
Point of Order	Y	Request a ruling from the Chair	The Chair shall either affirm the point of order or give a reason for denying the point of order.
Challenge to Ruling of the Chair	Y	To overturn a ruling from the Chair	During debate on a challenge, the Chair shall not preside. Speaker order: Chair, Challenger, not more than two additional members in favor of the ruling or the challenge. A majority is required to sustain the ruling of the Chair.
Orders of the Day	Y	Can only be called when the body is behind schedule	The body shall immediately proceed to a vote on all pending motions, and move to the scheduled agenda item.
Request for Information	N	Seeking clarification of the pending motion	Chair shall explain the pending motion.

Order of Precedence

	Interrupting?	Requires Vote?	Note:
Challenge to Ruling of the Chair	Y	Y	Majority to sustain the Ruling of the Chair
Point of Order	Y	N	The Chair shall either affirm the point of order or give a reason for denying the point of order.
Orders of the Day	Y	N	The body shall immediately proceed to a vote on all pending motions, and move to the scheduled agenda item.
Request for Information	N	N	Chair shall explain the pending motion.
Adjourn	N	Y	Unanimous Consent or 2/3
Substitute Motion	N	Y	Unanimous Consent or 2/3
Secondary Amendment	N	Y	Unanimous Consent or 2/3
Amendment	N	Y	Unanimous Consent or 2/3
Main Motion	N	Y	Unanimous Consent or majority
Suspension of the Rules	N	Y	Unanimous Consent or 2/3
Reconsider	N	Y	Unanimous Consent or 2/3

About the Authors

Author

Darryl W. Perry

Darryl was born and raised in Birmingham, AL and the surrounding area; graduating from Hewitt-Trussville High School in 1996. He graduated *summa cum laude* from New England College in 2022. He currently lives in Seattle, WA with his wife and cat, and is pursuing a J.D. from Seattle University School of Law in their Flex-hybrid program.

Darryl W. Perry has spent most of his adult life as an advocate & activist for peace and liberty. He was a public-interest lobbyist in New Hampshire from 2016-22, and worked with legislators on both sides of the aisle to pass legislation aimed as increasing personal liberty.

After law school, Darryl hopes to provide legal support to the wrongfully convicted, as well as defending nonviolent victimless offenders, and providing legal representation to people seeking to overturn unjust laws.

Honorary Co-Author

F. Mac Perry (aka Freddie Mac)

Darryl and his wife adopted Freddie Mac and his sister Fannie Mae as 10-year old orphans in early-2019. Freddie would often sit in Darryl's lap to observe, and help with, whatever he was doing. Freddie Mac attended zoom classes with Darryl, and after Darryl graduated form New England College, he was awarded a Certificate of Attendance.

Freddie attended Darryl's zoom classes at SU Law until his death on March 5, 2024 from renal failure.

Index

Other titles from Free Press Publications

ISBN13	Title
978-1-938357-21-3	*A Rebel's Journey*
978-1-938357-34-3	*Lapping Everyone on the Couch*
978-0-9842037-2-7	*The Anarcho Teachings of Yeshua*
978-1-938357-01-5	*The Diary of Henry Myers*
978-1-938357-30-5	*A Christmas Carol*
978-1-938357-13-8	*A Tale of Two Cities*
978-1-938357-29-9	*Adventures of Huckleberry Finn*
978-1-938357-08-4	*Alice's Adventures in Wonderland and Through the Looking-Glass*
978-1-938357-17-6	*An Essay on Trial by Jury*
978-1-938357-23-7	*Common Sense*
978-1-938357-31-2	*Lysistrata*
978-1-938357-36-7	*Moby Dick*
978-1-938357-04-6	*Narrative of the Life of Frederick Douglass, an American Slave, Written by Himself*
978-1-938357-27-5	*No Treason*
978-1-938357-28-2	*On Civil Disobedience and Life Without Principle*
978-1-938357-16-9	*Quote the Raven*
978-1-938357-15-2	*The Adventures of Tom Sawyer*
978-1-938357-10-7	*The Art of War*
978-1-938357-09-1	*The Awakening*
978-1-938357-24-4	*The Essential Emma Goldman*
978-1-938357-06-0	*The Jungle*
978-1-938357-25-1	*The Law*
978-1-938357-33-6	*The Life and Morals of Jesus of Nazareth*
978-1-938357-11-4	*The Republic*
978-1-938357-05-3	*The Scarlet Letter*
978-1-938357-07-7	*The Time Machine*
978-1-938357-20-6	*Travels into Several Remote Nations of the World in Four Parts*
978-1-938357-26-8	*What Is Man?*

PAGE INTENTIONALLY BLANK

PAGE INTENTIONALLY BLANK

PAGE INTENTIONALLY BLANK

PAGE INTENTIONALLY BLANK

PAGE INTENTIONALLY BLANK

PAGE INTENTIONALLY BLANK

PAGE INTENTIONALLY BLANK

Made in the USA
Las Vegas, NV
29 January 2026

4dbb8c23-1ea0-466c-8497-039c759537b9R01